1/12 8X   4 - 99   CRⅤ

NUBIAN KINGDOMS

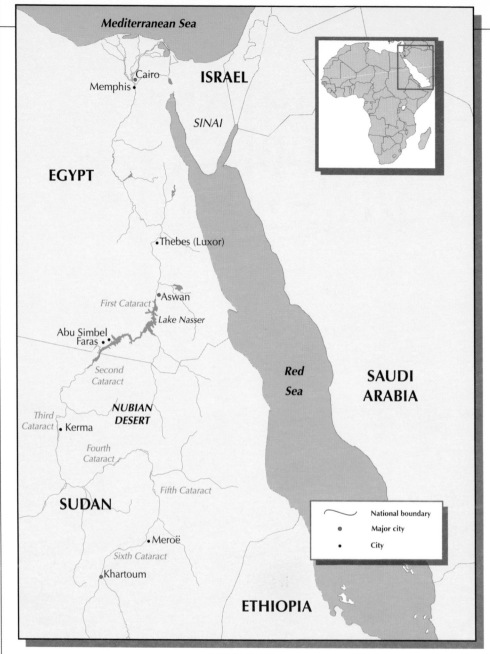

Mediterranean Sea

ISRAEL

Cairo
Memphis

SINAI

EGYPT

•Thebes (Luxor)

•Aswan
First Cataract
Lake Nasser
Abu Simbel
Faras

Second
Cataract

NUBIAN
DESERT

Third
Cataract •Kerma

Fourth
Cataract

Red
Sea

SAUDI
ARABIA

Fifth Cataract

SUDAN

•Meroë
Sixth Cataract
•Khartoum

ETHIOPIA

National boundary
Major city
City

Ancient Egypt and the kingdoms of ancient Nubia were trading partners, but they also competed for power in the Nile Valley for thousands of years.

~African Civilizations~

NUBIAN KINGDOMS

Edna R. Russmann, Ph.D.

A First Book

Franklin Watts
A Division of Grolier Publishing
New York / London / Hong Kong / Sydney
Danbury, Connecticut

Cover photo copyright ©: Werner Forman Archive/Art Resource, NY

Photographs copyright ©: Dave Bartruff/Corbis: p. 7; Paul Almasy/Corbis: pp. 9, 28; Roger Wood/Corbis: p. 10; Werner Forman Archive/Art Resource, NY: p. 13; Jonathan Blair/Corbis: p. 15; Dr. Edna R. Russmann: pp. 16, 18, 39, 44, 51, 54, 55; Trip/D. Maybury/The Viesti Collection: p. 21; Steve Kaufman/Corbis: p. 23; Museum of Fine Arts, courtesy of Dr. Tim Kendall: pp. 25, 27, 37, 49; Dr. Tim Kendall: pp. 31, 35, 47; Bojan Brecelj/Corbis: p. 42.

Library of Congress Cataloging-in-Publication Data

Russmann, Edna R.
   Nubian kingdoms / Edna Russman. — 1st ed.
     p.   cm. — (African civilizations)
   Includes bibliographical references and index.
   Summary: A survey of the history and culture of the North African Nubian kingdoms first settled by humans about 6000 B.C.
   ISBN 0-531-20283-6
   1. Nubia—History—Juvenile literature.   [1. Nubia—History.]
   I. Title. II. Series
   DT159.6.N83R88   1998
   939'.78—dc21   97-29389
                                            CIP
                                            AC

CONTENTS

INTRODUCTION

Nubia is the name of a region, not a country. The territory of Nubia begins at Khartoum, Sudan, where the Blue Nile River and the White Nile River join, and stretches north to the Egyptian city of Aswan. Nubia is named after the Nubians who live along this part of the Nile today, and whose ancestors lived there in ancient times.

In ancient times, Egypt's southern border was at Aswan, and Nubia was Egypt's southern neighbor. Today, the northern part of ancient Nubia forms the southern part of modern Egypt. The southern two-thirds of ancient Nubia now forms the northern part of the modern country of Sudan.

The Egyptians called Nubia Ta-nehesy (pronounced tah-NEH-heh-see), "the Southern Land."

Nubia is named after the Nubian people who live along the higher reaches of the Nile River. This Nubian boy is riding in a canoe.

They also knew it as Ta-sety (tah-SET-ee), "the Land of the Bow," because Nubian warriors were famous for their archery. The people of southern Nubia called their land Kush.

The study of ancient Nubia is a relatively new field. Until about twenty-five years ago, Nubian studies were little more than a minor branch of the study of ancient Egypt. The first major advance in the study of Nubia began in the 1950s, when Egypt announced its plan to build a new dam at Aswan. The dam would block the flow of the Nile, creating a huge lake that would fill most of the Nile Valley in northern Nubia and permanently flood Nubia's ancient remains. The United Nations appealed to the world for help in saving the Nubian monuments.

The very successful rescue operation that resulted is famous for moving the Egyptian temple of Abu Simbel, with its colossal statues of Ramesses II, from the bottom of the Nile valley to the top of the cliff several hundred feet above. Smaller Egyptian temples in this part of Nubia were also taken apart and rebuilt elsewhere. One, the Temple of Dendur, is now in the Metropolitan Museum of Art in New York. But the most important results of this opera-

Nubians wearing ancient dress in front of the temple of Abu Simbel which was constructed by Ramesses II in about 1250 B.C.

tion came from archaeologists—scientists who study how people lived long ago. Archaeological excavations of ancient Nubian towns and cemeteries in the region revealed for the first time just how rich and complex Nubia's history was.

Statue of Ramesses II in Wadi Sebua, Nubia

Since that time, archaeologists have been working in many parts of Nubia that were not flooded by the Aswan dam. The history of ancient Nubia is finally beginning to be written, but much work remains to be done, and many discoveries still lie ahead. For example, it was only in the 1980s and 1990s that excavations at Kerma revealed that it was once the capital of Kush.

Kerma, the first kingdom to rise to power in Kush, lasted from about 2400 to 1500 B.C. It is the oldest African kingdom yet known outside of Egypt. Kerma's wealth came from the valuable trade between Central Africa and Egypt. Kerma and Egypt competed for control of this trade. Kerma's defenses were strong, but around 1500 B.C. the Egyptians defeated the city and burned it.

For the next five centuries, the Egyptian army controlled almost all of ancient Nubia. After the end of the Egyptian occupation, however, a second kingdom of Kush rose to power. This kingdom lasted a long time, and its history is divided into two phases. During the first phase, beginning a little before 800 B.C., Napata was the capital of the kingdom. The Napatan kings conquered Egypt and ruled it from about 716 to 656 B.C. These Nubian kings considered themselves true *pharaohs*. They built their tombs, in the Kushite royal cemeteries near Napata, in the shape of *pyramids*. Long after they had been driven out of Egypt, they continued to call themselves kings of Egypt.

With time, however, the interests of the Napatan kings turned toward the south. Beginning about 590 B.C., they gradually moved their capital far to the south, to a city called Meroë (MAIR-oh-ee). The second, or Meroïtic (MAIR-oh-IT-ic), phase of the second kingdom of Kush is the most famous of the ancient African kingdoms, except for Egypt.

This second Kushite kingdom lasted nearly 1,200 years, from the first kings at Napata, before 800 B.C., to the fall of Meroë shortly before A.D. 350. By A.D. 340, however, Meroë had begun to decline. About this time it was defeated and perhaps destroyed by the kingdom of Aksum (AK-sum), to the west, in modern Ethiopia.

From the ruins of the Meroïtic kingdom, three smaller kingdoms arose: Ballana or Nobatia, Makuria, and Alwa. Far less is known about these kingdoms than the other Nubian kingdoms.

Egypt's effect on ancient Nubia was clear and often dramatic. Nubia's influence on Egypt is much harder to measure, but it too was great. Nubia was Egypt's main link to the rest of the African continent. It was both the channel through which Egypt received a large and vital part of its wealth, and

The rulers of the second kingdom of Kush were buried in small, steep pyramids.

Egypt's most important point of contact with a wide variety of other African cultures. Perhaps most important of all, Nubians in all periods were constantly immigrating into Egypt. Over the centuries, they undoubtedly enriched every aspect of Egyptian society. A small number of Nubian immigrants reached the top of Egyptian society, including pharaohs with Nubian ancestry.

ANCIENT NUBIA

Judging from a map, Nubia and Egypt are much alike. Both are desert lands through which the Nile River flows as a lifeline. But on the whole, Nubia is a harsher land. The winds blow harder in Nubia, and temperatures are more extreme. Farming in ancient Nubia was poorer than in Egypt, because the land watered by the Nile is often barren sand or rock—especially in northern Nubia. However, southern Nubia does receive a little rainfall each year.

THE NILE
In Egypt, the Nile flows north in a fairly straight line and without natural interruptions, providing a

Like Egypt, Nubia is a desert land. These Nubian women draw water from a well.

rapid and efficient means of transportation and communication. In Nubia, the river's course is much more winding. Along one long stretch, it almost reverses direction. The distance between Khartoum, Sudan, and Aswan, Egypt—about 600 miles (960 km) on the map—is almost doubled, to more than 1,100 miles (1,760 km), if one travels by river.

The Nubian Nile is interrupted by six large groups of rapids, called *cataracts*, which are numbered from north to south. The First Cataract is at

In Nubia the Nile is interrupted by rocky rapids, called cataracts. This view of part of the First Cataract, near Aswan, shows the rocks in the river.

Aswan, where it formed a natural boundary between Egypt and Nubia. The Sixth Cataract is a little north of Khartoum.

EARLY SETTLEMENTS

In Nubia, as in Egypt, archaeologists have found evidence of human settlements going back to 6000 B.C. and earlier. Information about these earliest Nile dwellers comes primarily from the figurines, jewelry, pottery, and weapons that they buried with their dead, apparently for use in the afterlife.

These artifacts differ in northern and southern Nubia—a fact that proves that there were several different groups of early peoples, each with their own culture. The artifacts also show that these early peoples traded with each other. For instance, some of the settlements in northern Nubia traded with southern Egypt, showing that Nubia and Egypt were in contact from very early times.

THE A-GROUP PEOPLE

By about 3500 B.C., a group of people—known by scholars as the A-group people—were living in northern Nubia. These people made human and animal figures in clay and attractive conical cups with red designs painted on pale tan pottery. They mined gold and traded with peoples living north of the First Cataract, in what would later be Egypt.

By 3100 B.C., the A-group people were building large, ornate graves for their leaders. This suggests that their leaders were becoming as rich and important as kings, and that the A-group settlements were close to being united into a kingdom. To the north, in what was soon to be Egypt, the same sort of thing was happening at the same time:

Nubian pot with ostrich design made by the A-group people

Communities were combining into ever larger units, and their leaders were becoming more and more like kings.

In about 3100 B.C., northern and southern Egypt were united into a single kingdom, under the kings of the First *Dynasty*, or royal family.

This milestone in Egyptian history was almost as important for Nubia, because the First Dynasty kings immediately started leading military raids into Nubia against the A-group people.

EGYPTIAN CONTROL

We cannot be sure that the Egyptian campaigns were intended to prevent the rise of a rival kingdom in Nubia, but they had that effect. Within a very short time the A-group people seem to have disappeared from northern Nubia. Scholars are not sure what became of them. Some may have fled south to the Second Cataract, others even farther, to Kerma. Never again during the pharaohs' rule of Egypt did a Nubian kingdom arise in northern Nubia.

Nubia and Egypt were in constant contact throughout the ancient period. Egypt, the more powerful of the two, was usually the aggressor and often had troops stationed in Nubia. The Egyptian presence brought the influences of Egyptian culture and religion to Nubia, while effectively serving to *inhibit* the development of strong Nubian states.

Ancient Egypt's activities in Nubia were not only based on fending off Nubian military attacks—although Nubian archers could, and sometimes did, threaten the Aswan border. Nubia had two things that Egypt *coveted*. The first was the mineral wealth, especially gold, buried in Nubia's deserts. Even more important was Nubia's strategic location between Egypt and Central Africa—the source of Egypt's trade in leopard skins and elephant tusks, live giraffes and monkeys, ebony, ostrich plumes, and much of its gold. Whether these goods traveled down the Nile or along caravan routes through the desert, they could reach Egypt only by passing through Nubia. Egypt was determined to control that trade.

Following the First Dynasty, the pharaohs of the Old Kingdom (about 2649 to 2150 B.C.) sent expeditions of workmen to Nubia to quarry rare stones and to mine gold. The *nobles* of Aswan governed the border for the pharaohs. They supervised the military control of northern Nubia and also the trade coming up through Nubia from Central Africa. Several of them left written accounts of their careers on the walls of their tombs. These *hieroglyphic* inscriptions record their many trips into Nubia and their dealings with different Nubian peoples, both allies and enemies.

Graves of Egyptian nobles in Nubia

During the Middle Kingdom (about 2134–1797 B.C.), Egypt extended its power in Nubia farther to the south. Egypt established a permanent presence by building a series of enormous forts, made of mud brick. They were placed at strategic points along the Nubian Nile. The main job of the Egyptian troops in Nubia was to control trade along the Nile and the desert caravan routes through Nubia. But the massive size and heavy defenses of the forts suggest that Egypt was also concerned about the growth of another power even farther south: Kerma, in Kush.

2 KERMA

Kerma, the first kingdom of Kush, flourished from about 2400 to 1500 B.C. At its peak, it controlled most of Nubia, from the border with Egypt at Aswan to as far south as the Fourth Cataract, upriver from Gebel Barkal. Its influence, however, extended even farther—south to the borders of present-day Ethiopia and west into the Sahara Desert for several hundred miles. In part, the extent of this territory was possible because Egypt had grown weak.

KERMA

The capital of the Kushite kingdom was located on the Nile, just south of the Third Cataract. Today,

A view of the Gebel Barkal region

the ruins of this city lie near, and partly under, the present-day town of Kerma. Since the name of the ancient Kushite city is not known, it too is called Kerma, and archaeologists often refer to its ancient society as the Kerma culture.

In the desert outside present-day Kerma stand the impressive remains of two huge structures, built of sun-dried mud brick. The people of Kerma call them *deffufas* (deh-FOO-fahs), which is a modern Nubian word for tall mud-brick buildings. Both the local residents and the few Western travelers who ventured that far up the Nile before the twentieth century realized that the *deffufas* must be very old. But no one knew when they were built, who built them, or why.

DISCOVERIES AT KERMA

Between 1913 and 1916, American archaeologist George Reisner excavated in and around the Kerma *deffufas*. In a large cemetery nearby he found several gigantic circular tombs that were undoubtedly made for important rulers. Even though these tombs had been broken into by thieves in ancient times, they still contained remarkable objects.

Beautiful plaques representing animals were among the archaeological finds at Kerma.

The finds at Kerma included the remains of richly ornamented beds on which the kings had been laid to rest, and superb jewelry, including large, round beads of blue-glazed crystal that look like glass (which had not yet been invented). Also discovered were animal-shaped plaques carved in bone, which had been used for decorating furniture, and glittery flakes of mica, used for sewing onto caps.

Also found in these tombs and in other, smaller tombs at Kerma were large quantities of red clay pots that are almost as thin and hard as china. These included hundreds of round "Kerma cups," each topped with a distinctive band of shiny black graphite.

Some of the Kerma tombs also contained Egyptian statues of kings and nobles that had been made for Egyptian tombs and temples. Scholars were puzzled to find them in Nubian royal tombs. However, the statues were dated to between 2000 and 1700 B.C., which proved that the Kerma culture was very old and had interacted with Egypt.

EGYPT LEAVES NUBIA

Egypt suffered a political collapse shortly after 1800 B.C. It withdrew its forces from Nubia and abandoned the great Nile forts. Weakened, Egypt was conquered by foreigners from the east, in present-day Lebanon and Syria, whom the Egyptians called *Hyksos*.

Egypt's withdrawal created a power vacuum in Nubia. The Kushite rulers at Kerma took full advantage of this. From 1750 to 1580 B.C., the Kerma kingdom expanded greatly. The Kushites took over some of the abandoned Egyptian forts, and, to the Egyptians' fury, they allied themselves with the Hyksos. This alliance may explain the presence of the Egyptian statues at Kerma: Perhaps it was the Hyksos or their allies who looted Egyptian tombs and temples and sent the statues

A Kerma pot decorated with a hippopotamus head

to the kings of Kush. The items may have been pre-sented as royal gifts, or they may have been pres-tige imports—with prices to match.

RECENT DISCOVERIES

In the last twenty years, archaeologists have made many new discoveries in the Kerma region. They have shown that most of the people of Kush were herders of cattle and sheep and lived in small rural communities. But Kerma—the most ancient African city yet discovered outside of Egypt—was

A mud house in Nubia

a great walled city. Its massive mud-brick walls and fortified towers rested on stone foundations and were surrounded by a dry moat.

Outside the walls lay villages, farms that provided food for the city, and, at the Nile's edge, a port with official warehouses.

Inside Kerma's walls, about two thousand people lived and worked in a mix of official buildings, private homes, workshops, and even small farms. The mud-brick houses were built around inner, open-air courtyards. Large outer courtyards, shared by the inhabitants of several houses—probably members of an extended family—were used as cattle pens and as a place for making handicrafts and preparing food.

A special room in the home was set apart for worship and other family gatherings. In parts of Sudan today, many homes still have rooms or open spaces where the family gather to pray and to conduct family business. This is one of many ancient Nubian customs that have survived into the present.

THE RULERS OF KERMA

We do not know what the rulers of the first kingdom of Kush were called or how they were chosen. But archaeologists have discovered their palace at Kerma.

Other important royal functions probably took place in another building at Kerma: a large circular building, at least 30 feet (10 m) high, that stood within its own walled enclosure. The interior of this tower-like building was dominated by a single room, 36 feet (12 m) square, where the king probably received his subjects and foreign visitors. In the early twentieth century, similar reception halls were still in use in southern Sudan and in other Central African states.

THE DEFFUFAS

Archaeologists have shown that Kerma's mysterious *deffufas* were in fact temples. The larger one, the western *deffufa*, was the city's main temple. It stood within its own compound, inside the city walls. Even in its ruined state, this enormous structure, 156 x 78 feet (52 x 26 m) in area and 52.5 feet (17.5 m) high, is visible for miles around. The inside is an almost solid mass of mud brick. A staircase at the entrance leads to a small room, which opens onto a dead-end corridor. This curious passage is 21 feet (7 m) long, but only 18 inches (0.5 m) wide. Since it is in the heart of the temple, it may have been the sanctuary of the city's main god or goddess.

The eastern *deffufa* was a funerary temple in which prayers and offerings were made for the occupant of one of the great royal tombs. The walls of its two rooms were lined with blue-glazed tiles and gold leaf. A smaller funerary temple connected with another of the royal tombs had walls covered

One of two ancient deffufas at Kerma

with painted scenes of men fishing, bulls fighting, and row upon row of hippopotami.

TRADE

Kerma's wealth was based on its control of the trade between Central Africa and Egypt. This, in turn, was based on controlling the trade routes through the desert and, especially, along the Nile. Although Kerma's port was washed away by the Nile long ago, part of one administrative building has survived. Inside, archaeologists have found broken labels written in Egyptian hieroglyphs. These labels came from the seals on packages of goods imported from Egypt. Since the Kushites had no written language of their own, they apparently hired Egyptians to keep their trade accounts and inventories.

Egypt was Kerma's most important trading partner, but it was also a competitor and, above all, a potential enemy. The first kingdom of Kush flourished while Egypt was under the rule of the Hyksos and could not threaten Nubia. But around 1550 B.C., an Egyptian prince finally drove out the Hyksos. Fifty years later, Egypt set out to reconquer Nubia. Its prime target was Kush.

EGYPTIAN CONQUEST

Moving south along the Nile, the Egyptians rebuilt and reoccupied their old forts. This time, however, they pushed farther south into Nubia than ever before, until they reached Kerma. The Egyptians broke through Kerma's massive walls and destroyed the western *deffufa* and other buildings by fire. The defeat and the destruction were catastrophic—the first kingdom of Kush ceased to exist.

3 NAPATA

When the Egyptians reconquered Nubia in about 1500 B.C., they were determined to crush Kushite power completely. After the fall of Kerma, they marched southward to Gebel Barkal, near the Fourth Cataract. They established their stronghold in a nearby city called Napata. Napata and Gebel Barkal marked the southernmost extent of the Egyptian penetration of Nubia.

The exact location of ancient Napata has not been discovered, so virtually nothing is known about it. It is even unclear whether it was a Kushite town or built by Egyptians. Gebel Barkal, however, has been studied.

GEBEL BARKAL

Gebel Barkal is an isolated *mesa* that rises dramatically from the desert. This striking landmark was probably sacred to the Kushites. Its modern name, Gebel Barkal, is Arabic for "Blessed Mountain." The ancient Egyptians called it Djew Wab, which has almost the same meaning.

Several Egyptian kings emphasized Gebel Barkal's religious importance by building temples at the foot of its cliff. These temples were dedicated to the great Egyptian state god, Amun. In Egypt, Amun was usually shown in human form, but at Gebel Barkal he was more often represented as a ram or a ram-headed man. For this reason, the ram's head also became an emblem of Kushite kings.

EGYPTIAN OCCUPATION OF NUBIA

Throughout the period known as the Egyptian New Kingdom (about 1550–1070 B.C.), Egypt remained in Nubia. This was the Egyptians' longest and most intensive occupation. All along the Nubian Nile, they built temples to Amun and other gods, including the temple of Abu Simbel, which was constructed by Ramesses II in about 1250 B.C.

View of Gebel Barkal with a ram-headed sphinx, or criosphinx, in the foreground. The criosphinx, now hornless, represents the god Amun.

Along with the Egyptian priests who came to serve in these temples, Egypt sent many other Egyptians to live in Nubia as soldiers, officials, and traders. They brought with them their language, religion, and customs. Some of the children of high-ranking Nubians were sent to the Egyptian royal court to be educated in Egyptian ways. These children were like hostages: If their fathers were not loyal to Egypt, they might never see their children again.

A SECOND KINGDOM OF KUSH

The Egyptians pulled out of Nubia again in about 1000 B.C., this time because of political and economic problems at home. With their departure, written information about Nubia during the next two hundred years practically disappears. By 800 B.C., however, a Kushite royal family from Napata was in control of southern Nubia. For the second time, a powerful kingdom had risen in Kush.

The people of this second kingdom of Kush were almost certainly of the same *ethnicity* as those of the first. But seven hundred years had passed since the fall of Kerma, and the long Egyptian occupation had influenced the Kushites. The new

A criosphinx in honor of Amun, decorated with precious stones

Kushite capital, Napata, had formerly been Egypt's southernmost stronghold. It was also the center of the Nubian *cult* of the Egyptian god Amun, who was worshiped in the temples that the Egyptians had built at Gebel Barkal. Although the rulers of Napata worshiped Kushite gods—such as Apedemak (pronounced ah-PEH-deh-mack), a war god represented in the form of a lion or a lion-headed man—they also worshiped Egyptian gods, including Osiris and Isis. But above all, they were devoted to the ram-headed Amun of Gebel Barkal, whom they considered their family god.

THE KUSHITE INVASIONS OF EGYPT

After they gained control of Nubia, the rulers of Napata came to believe that Amun wanted them to rule Egypt. Around 760 B.C., the Kushite king Kashta (which means "the Kushite") invaded Egypt. He established his power from Aswan northward, possibly as far as Thebes. But it was Kashta's successor, Piye (pronounced PEE-yeh; also spelled Piankhy, pronounced PEE-ankh-ee), who first invaded all of Egypt and brought it under Kushite rule, in about 725 B.C.

Egypt had been ripe for a takeover. For more than a century, the power of the pharaohs had been declining, until finally the northern part of Egypt was divided among half a dozen local rulers. Some of these minor rulers called themselves pharaohs, but most had power over only one city. Southern Egypt, including Thebes and Aswan, had become practically independent of any royal government. Many southern Egyptians were willing to accept a Kushite pharaoh because Nubia and southern Egypt shared a special devotion to Amun. Also, many southern Egyptians had Nubian relatives or ancestors.

The top of the great slab describing Piye's conquest of Egypt shows the god Amun seated before Piye's enemies, who bow down on either side of him. The figure of Piye, which once stood directly in front of Amun, has been erased.

Piye's conquest of Egypt is described on a huge granite slab that was erected in Amun's temple at Gebel Barkal. This slab, which is now in Cairo, is 70 inches (1.8 m) high, 70.5 inches (1.84 m) wide, and 17 inches (0.43 m) thick. The inscription is carved on all four sides. Like all the Napatan inscriptions, it is written in hieroglyphs, the language of the ancient Egyptians. It describes how Piye moved northward, defeating some of the minor Egyptian rulers and frightening others into surrender.

At the ancient Egyptian capital of Memphis, Piye won a decisive victory over the coalition of northern rulers. He celebrated by going to worship the Egyptian sun god Ra, whose temple was near Memphis. Piye then received the conquered rulers, who bowed down to the ground before him and swore oaths of loyalty. Piye apparently believed them and went back home to Napata.

THE TWENTY-FIFTH DYNASTY OF EGYPT

No sooner had Piye left Egypt than the conquered northern rulers began to reassert themselves. In about 716 B.C., Piye's successor, Shabaka (SHAH-bah-kah), had to conquer northern Egypt all over again. Realizing that Egypt could not be controlled from outside, Shabaka took up residence within it, probably at Memphis. He and his successors, Shebitku (sheh-BIT-koo), Taharqa (tah-HAR-kah), and Tantamani (tahn-tah-MAH-nee), ruled Egypt until 656 B.C. This family of Kushite pharaohs is known in Egyptian records as the Twenty-fifth Dynasty.

Shabaka and his successors continued to be rulers of Kush, but they kept their two kingdoms separate—perhaps to preserve the Kushite heritage of which they were proud. Though the Kushite pharaohs were not able to spend much time in their homeland, they always considered Kush their home. Upon their deaths, their bodies were returned to Kush for burial in the royal cemeteries near Napata and Gebel Barkal.

The tombs of the Kushite pharaohs, unlike the mound-shaped graves of their ancestors, were now built in the form of Egyptian pyramids, but they were smaller and steeper than the much older Egyptian royal pyramids. Inside the Kushite pyramids, the mummified remains of the kings were laid not on the traditional Kushite beds but in great *sarcophagi* decorated with Egyptian gods and hieroglyphic inscriptions.

As the rulers of two lands with different traditions, the Kushite pharaohs had a sense of their complex identity. Since they believed that Amun had made them true kings of Egypt, they had themselves represented in the traditional poses, costumes, and crowns of Egyptian kings. However, they never pretended to be Egyptian. In both Egypt and Nubia, their images included non-Egyptian features, such as broad, round heads, fleshy cheeks and nostrils, and massive, columnar necks. They wore

A Napatan pyramid near Kerma

earrings and necklaces decorated with the ram's head of Amun's cult at Gebel Barkal. And often, instead of Egyptian crowns, they wore a traditional Kushite headdress, a broad headband, which was tied over their short-cropped hair.

The Kushite Twenty-fifth Dynasty was a period of wealth and creativity in both Kush and Egypt. The pharaohs built temples for the gods of both lands. The greatest Kushite pharaoh, Taharqa, was also the greatest builder, especially in honor of Amun. In Kush, he built large temples for Amun at Gebel Barkal and other places. Most of his many additions to the temple of Amun at Karnak in Egypt have been destroyed. However, just inside the entrance still stands the "Taharqa column," the remains of a monumental gateway.

THE ASSYRIANS

Like most Egyptian kings, the Kushite pharaohs were involved in international politics. They sent their army into the Middle East to support their allies—the small kingdoms of Sidon, Ashkelon, and Judah—against the Assyrians, who were one of the most warlike powers of antiquity. The Assyrian king Sennacherib warned King Hezekiah of Judah against relying on Taharqa. In the Bible, Sennacherib is quoted as calling Egypt and Taharqa a broken reed of a staff, "which will pierce the hand of anyone who leans on it" (II Kings 18: 21–22).

Portrait head of Taharqa

The Assyrians eventually invaded Egypt from the north in 671 B.C., forcing Taharqa to flee before them. Reaching Memphis, they captured some of Taharqa's family, including the crown prince.

A second Assyrian invasion in 665 B.C. penetrated southward to Thebes. Taharqa died shortly after the second invasion. His successor, Tanta-mani, tried to regain control of Egypt, but the Assyrians returned in 663 B.C. and chased Tanta-mani as far south as Thebes. This time, they did not merely plunder Egypt as before; they also burned and destroyed, not sparing even the temples. Tantamani fled to Kush.

The local rulers in northern Egypt were as unhappy under Assyrian rule as they had been under the Kushites. They soon invited Tantamani back to Egypt. But in the end, the Assyrian army was too great a threat. In 656 B.C., Tantamani went back to Kush. He never returned to Egypt, nor did any of his successors. For many years, however, they continued to call themselves kings of Egypt, although they ruled only in Nubia. They contin-ued to use Egyptian crowns, pyramid tombs, and other Egyptian royal symbols. Amun remained their family god. As time passed, these Egyptian traditions were adapted to Kushite customs and beliefs, until they became fully Kushite.

4 MEROË

Tantamani's successors at Napata gradually turned their attention southward. They moved the capital south to the city of Meroë, between the Fifth and Sixth Cataracts. This stage of the second kingdom of Kush is therefore usually called the kingdom of Meroë. Meroë is the most famous of the ancient Nubian states, but it was in fact a continuation of the second kingdom of Kush—a Meroïtic phase.

MEROÏTIC WRITING
While the Kushites ruled Egypt, and for a short time afterward, educated Nubians learned the Egyptian language in addition to their own, and wrote Egyptian in hieroglyphs.

A view of a pyramid and a section of wall in a royal cemetery

After their separation from Egypt, the people of Nubia began to write their own language. At first they adapted the Egyptian hieroglyphs, but later they developed their own alphabet. Meroïtic is the oldest known written language in Africa, outside of Egypt. Unfortunately, no one has yet been able to decipher it, partly because the language has died out, leaving very few clues to its meanings. We cannot read the many inscriptions on the temples and royal tombs of the Meroïtic period.

RULERS OF MEROË

Unlike Egypt—where relatively few women, such as Hatshepsut and Cleopatra, ever governed—a number of queens ruled at Meroë. A Kushite queen was called a *candace* (pronounced kan-DAH-kay). When rumors of these *candaces* reached ancient Greece and Rome, they caused surprise, because women there had no role in public or political life.

What we know about the kings and queens of Meroë comes mainly from representations of them on temple walls and in the small chapels attached to their pyramid tombs. These show kings as plump, and queens as very fat. It seems that the more important a man or woman was, the fatter he or especially she was expected to be.

Kushite rulers regarded their kingdom as including all of Nubia, although Meroë lay very far south. But ancient Egypt—even when it was ruled by the Greeks and Romans—always wanted control of northern Nubia. The disputed territory of northern Nubia often caused friction between Egypt and Meroë, but the two countries occasionally sent each other diplomats.

The wide variety of goods found at Meroë suggests that the kingdom traded widely. This pot shows two crocodiles fighting.

LIFE AT MEROË

Regardless of political tensions, the trade between Nubia and Egypt always continued. Meroë sent to Egypt gold, ivory, exotic woods, and other products from Central Africa, including elephants, which were used in battle as an ancient version of the tank. Through their trading network, the Kushites acquired Greek and Roman statues, glassware, and other luxury objects, all of which have been found at Meroë.

At its height, Meroë may have had as many as 25,000 inhabitants. Archaeologists have not yet excavated much in the city itself, but the walled-off palace area, several temples, and the cemeteries are well preserved. A number of smaller Meroïtic cities, with their own temples and cemeteries, are also known. Most people, however, lived in country villages, where they grew the crops and tended the animals that fed the larger population.

THE GOLD OF MEROË

The wealth of Meroë and the brilliance of its civilization are perhaps best shown by a treasure of gold and enamel jewelry that belonged to the *candace* Amanishakheto (ah-mahn-ee-shah-KAY-toe), who lived sometime around 10 B.C. Her jewels, mostly rings and bracelets, were buried with the queen in her pyramid tomb in the royal cemetery of Meroë. They remained there undisturbed until 1834, when an Italian adventurer named Giuseppe Ferlini visited the cemetery and broke into her burial chamber.

The importance of preserving archaeological

This scorpion sculpture would have been of little value to treasure hunters searching for gold in Meroë. Today it is considered an important example of Meroïtic art.

information by using proper excavation techniques was not understood in Ferlini's day. In his greed for treasure, Ferlini destroyed a great deal of evidence that could have provided precious information about Meroë. He sold the looted treasures to two German museums, where they are still on view today.

Hoping to return to Meroë and find more gold, Ferlini lied about where he had found the treasure. Instead of admitting that it was in the underground burial chamber with Amanishakheto's remains, he said that it had been in a secret room at the top of her pyramid. Ferlini's story was believed because nobody then knew that the Kushite pyramids were solid—unlike most Egyptian royal pyramids. Ferlini never returned to Nubia, but—thanks to his story and the greed of other would-be tomb robbers—almost every Kushite royal pyramid in the cemeteries of both Meroë and Napata soon lost its top.

DECLINE

The economy of Meroë declined when the Roman rulers of Egypt switched their trading contacts from the Nile Valley to the Red Sea coast, far to the east. At the same time, new settlers, the Noba people, began moving into the Nile Valley from the west. Then, in about A.D. 340, Meroë itself was invaded by the king of Aksum, in present-day Ethiopia. Meroë never recovered from this blow, which may have put an end to the long line of Kushite rulers.

5 THE LATE NUBIAN KINGDOMS

In the power vacuum left by the collapse of the second kingdom of Kush in the fourth century B.C., another kingdom emerged in northern Nubia. Its kings and queens were buried in enormous tombs, together with silver crowns decorated with large garnets, elaborate metal lamps and incense burners, ornate horse trappings, and other rich grave goods.

Some archaeologists call the people of this later kingdom the Ballana (bah-LAH-nah) culture, after the modern name for the site of one of the royal cemeteries. Another, and perhaps a better, name for them is post-Meroïtic, because the precious objects in their royal tombs were clearly derived from

A silver crown from the late Nubian kingdom of Ballana. The ram's head links the crown to earlier Nubian kingdoms. The cutout shapes along the top rim of the crown represent cobras—a sign of royalty in Egypt—with sun disks on their heads.

objects made for the kings and queens buried at Meroë. Some scholars think refugees from Meroë founded the Ballana kingdom. They were joined by Noba immigrants coming into Kush from the west. Over time, the Nubian languages spoken by these newcomers replaced the language of the Kushite people.

Top view of a playful oil lamp in the form of a human head. The eyes are made of inlaid metal and glass.

As in all the Nubian kingdoms, the wealth of this kingdom came from trade. The Ballana kings, however, concentrated on the caravan routes through the desert. This may be because they were the first to make extensive use of camels, which are much more efficient desert travelers than donkeys.

Very little is known about the Ballana kingdom before the fifth century A.D., when one of its kings was named Silko. In the sixth century, the kingdom was called Nobatia (no-BAH-tee-ah). Its capital was near Ballana, at the modern town of Faras.

By the sixth century, two other kingdoms existed south of Nobatia: Makuria (mah-KOO-ree-ah), in the middle of Nubia, and Alwa (AHL-wah), farther to the south, with its capital near Khartoum.

Nobatia was converted to Christianity in A.D. 543, Makuria, in A.D. 570, and Alwa, in A.D. 580. Nobatia's cathedral was built in Faras. The ruins of this cathedral were excavated in the 1970s. Many fine paintings were preserved on the walls, including representations of the bishops and biblical subjects, such as the three men in the fiery furnace and the Nativity.

In the seventh century A.D. Egypt was conquered by Arab Muslims. The Arab invaders continued south to Nubia, but there were defeated twice. The Nubians and Arabs then signed a treaty, which remained in effect for six hundred years. The treaty allowed the Nubian kingdoms to retain their independence and remain Christian long after Egypt had become a Muslim country.

From the thirteenth century on, however, the late Nubian kingdoms weakened, and the Muslim rulers of Egypt began to advance into Nubia.

Nobatia was the last kingdom to hold out against the invaders, but by the fifteenth century A.D. it too had disappeared. Nubia became, as it remains today, predominantly Arabic-speaking and Muslim in religion.

NUBIA TODAY

The Nubian languages of the Noba people are still spoken in the Nubian Nile Valley. The Noba people have given their name to the modern Nubians, and to Nubia itself.

Along with Egypt, Nubia provides the most ancient evidence for African kingship, urban settlement, writing, and art. Both Egypt and Nubia would have been very different places if the other had not existed. Together, they provide a unique view of international relations at the beginning of African history.

TIMELINE

Approximate date	NUBIA	EGYPT
5500–3300 B.C.	Earliest Nubian cultures	Predynastic
3500	Rise of A-group	
3100	Egyptian raids into Nubia	First Dynasty
3000	A-group disappears	
2649–2150	Egyptian trade and mines	Old Kingdom
2400	Rise of Kerma	
2060–1633	Egyptian forts in Nubia	Middle Kingdom
1786–1550	Egyptians leave Nubia; Kerma and Hyksos allied	Hyksos rule Egypt
1750–1580	Kerma expands throughout Nubia	
1550	Hyksos expelled	
1550–1070	Egypt returns to Nubia	New Kingdom
1500	Destruction and fall of Kerma	
1479–1425	Building of temple of Amun at Gebel Barkal	Thutmose III
1290–1224	Temple of Abu Simbel built	Ramesses II
1000	Egypt leaves Nubia	
800	Rise of Kushite dynasty at Napata	
760	Kashta invades Egypt	
725	Piye conquers Egypt	

Approximate date	NUBIA	EGYPT
716 B.C.	Shabaka reconquers Egypt	
716–656	Kushites rule Egypt	25th Dynasty (Kushite)
690–664	Taharqa	Taharqa
671–663	Three Assyrian invasions	
656	Tantamani flees to Napata	End of 25th Dynasty
590	Capital shifts to Meroë	
332–30		Greece rules Egypt
30 B.C.–A.D. 395		Rome rules Egypt
10 B.C.	Candace Amanishakheto buried at Meroë	
A.D. 340	Meroë falls to Aksum; rise of Ballana kingdom	
450–642		Byzantium rules Egypt
after 500	Kingdoms of Nobatia, Makuria, and Alwa emerge	
543–580	Nobatia, Makuria, and Alwa become Christian	
642	Nubia repels Arab invasion	Arab conquest
after 1200	Local rulers adopt Islam	
after 1400	Nobatia is conquered by Arab Muslims	

GLOSSARY

candace Meroïtic queen

cataract steep rapids in a river

covet to wish for enviously

cult system of religious beliefs and ritual

deffufa tall mud-brick building

dynasty powerful family that rules for generations

ethnicity classification of a large group of people on the basis of a common national, racial, religious, linguistic, or cultural quality

hieroglyphic picture-script system of writing used in ancient Egypt

Hyksos ancient Egyptian name for people from present-day Lebanon and Syria, who ruled Egypt 1750–1550 B.C.

inhibit hold in check; restrain

mesa isolated flat-topped natural elevation

noble a person of high birth or rank

pharaoh ruler of ancient Egypt

pyramid ancient Egyptian structure that rises from a square base to a point; used as a tomb for a pharaoh

sarcophagus (plural: sarcophagi) coffin made of stone

FOR FURTHER READING

Kendall, Timothy. "Kingdom of Kush." *National Geographic* 178/5 (November 1990), pp. 96-125.

Mann, Kenny. *Egypt, Kush, Aksum: Northeast Africa.* Parsippany, NJ: Dillon Press, 1997.

FOR ADVANCED READERS

Adams, William Y. *Nubia: Corridor to Africa.* London, Princeton, NJ: Allen Lane/Princeton University Press, (1977) 1984.

Hintze, Fritz and Ursula. *Civilizations of the Old Sudan: Kerma. Kush. Christian Nubia.* Leipzig-Amsterdam: Edition Leipzig, 1968.

WEB SITES

Due to the changeable nature of the Internet, sites appear and disappear very quickly. Internet addresses must be entered with capital and lowercase letters exactly as they appear.

Gateway of Nubia:
    http://uts.cc.utexas.edu/~rocman/index.htm

Images from History:
    http://www.hartford-hwp.com/ image_archive/index.html

Northwestern University Library—History of Ancient Egypt:
    http://www.library.nwu.edu/class/history/B94/

INDEX

ABOUT THE AUTHOR

Edna R. Russmann, Ph.D., is a specialist on ancient Egyptian and Kushite art. She has served as a museum curator at the Boston Museum of Fine Arts and the Metropolitan Museum of Art. She is currently a research associate at the Brooklyn Museum of Art. Russmann has taught at a number of universities and has lectured extensively. She is the author of the book *Egyptian Sculpture: Cairo and Luxor.* In addition, she has written many scholarly works and other works for the general public.